THE MANAGER'S SURVIVAL GUIDE

TERRI MALINSKI

DEDICATION

To my family for always supporting me.

CONTENTS

ACKNOWLEDGMENTS

I never would have considered writing this book if it hadn't been for Raymond Aaron who inspired me with his transformational thinking during a seminar I attended. My thanks also go out to Jay Smith, who was one of the best management mentors I ever had and taught me how to handle people and resources and to my good friend Shannon Smith who helped with the editing and helped me organize my thoughts.

1 WHAT IS A MANAGER

Before we delve into surviving as a manager, let's take a step back and actually look at the dictionary definition of management. What is this beast? We need to understand what we're dealing with before we can tackle it.

According to the Merriam-Webster dictionary, the word '*management*' means:

1: the act or art of managing: the conducting or supervising of something (as a business)
2: judicious use of means to accomplish an end
3: the collective body of those who manage or direct an enterprise

and '*Manager*' means:

1: one that manages: as a**)** a person who conducts business or household affairs b): a person whose work or profession is management 2: a person who directs a team or athlete 3: a student who in scholastic or collegiate sports supervises equipment and records under the direction of a coach[1]

---

[1]   http://www.merriam-webster.com/dictionary/manager

So why is this important? Because many people don't really understand what a manager is or does and why management is important. They think the manager is simply the guy or gal with the whip, badgering and threatening them to get the job done (and that they probably could do a better job without them).

For most people, their manager is simply a necessary evil and one they'd prefer to avoid at all costs. How many of us have panicked when the boss called us into his office saying 'we need to talk'? It's like being called to the principal's office when we've done something bad. That's why many people have a very negative impression of a manager. But in reality, that's not a manager's function.

Think of a manager as an orchestra conductor. She's given a piece of music to play (the strategic plan). How to play that music (execute the strategic plan) is her job. She has various musicians (project leads and project managers) and musical instruments (the people in the organization doing the actual work) in the orchestra (department or departments throughout the organization) and must conduct them efficiently and in harmony to achieve the precise sound of the music they are playing (achieve the strategic goals of the department).

When the sound is off on an instrument (the team is straying from the strategic plan), it's her duty as the conductor to let the musician (project manager) know ("we need to talk"), so the instrument can be put back into tune (get back on track to the strategic plan) or replaced (personnel changed) if the sound is not harmonizing with the rest of the music.

Thus, the manager is the person who takes the strategic goals of the company and figures out how to execute them within her organization. As such, that doesn't take a master's degree nor a PhD (despite what some corporations seem to think these days). What it does take is the ability to be a visionary and articulate that vision clearly. You must be able to take a business strategy, explain it clearly to your team, motivate them, execute your strategy and get outrageous results when done.

Let me give you an example from my own experience. In the IT department, the strategic decision was made to rewrite an accounts payable system that I was in charge with maintaining. The system had become cumbersome, inaccurate, and difficult to easily modify as regulatory changes were issued. Changes and rewrites to the system had been attempted in the past with disastrous results. The last attempted rewrite went horribly over budget and the rewrite became totally unworkable.

I had come into the group as the director at the tail end of the last disastrous attempt to rewrite the system. The team was floundering, demoralized and the customer as well as senior management had become frustrated with the progress.

Normally, the first thing someone would do is take the current project and just try to fix it. Instead, I went to the customer and asked for her five year strategy. What did she REALLY want the system to do for her? If she could have her ideal system, what would it do? What I found out was that the rewrite that had failed, wasn't even going to give her what she really needed the system to do. It was a case, (and unfortunately, in IT, all-to-frequent), of the IT department thinking they know the business needs of the business customers better than the actual customer. That's a serious and conceited mistake.

After getting the customer's input on what she really needed the system to do, I went to senior management and asked the same questions. I also asked them realistically, what were they willing to spend on a rewrite. Having a strategic plan is great, but if there's no way you can get it funded, it's useless.

Next, I went through the existing project proposal and plans, and after reviewing everything, I threw it all out and called a team meeting. We went back to square one. I gave them the vision from the customer, what help we could expect realistically from senior management and based upon my knowledge of the team and the strategic vision of the department, and what I felt we realistically could accomplish. I asked for opinions from those that knew the current system well and sat down with my acting project manager and formulated a different way of achieving the goal. I also knew that the IT department would be outsourcing in the next few years, so the new system would have to be easy to maintain, both now and in the future.

The entire system was broken into component chunks which would be much more manageable to rewrite than trying to do the entire system in one go. The team member most familiar with that piece of the system was put in charge of the rewrite of that component. In effect, they became mini-managers or supervisors of that component. Once we determined in what order components had to be completed before being reintegrated into the complete system, the project was turned over to a project manager to break each component into individual tasks and then schedule them.

By breaking the system into components, getting a realistic vision from the customer and senior management, I knew what we could and should accomplish. The new rewrite project was handled by the project manager leaving me free to attend to other duties. When she had an issue with specific tasks, I mentored her and handled the personnel issues, leaving her free to do her job of managing the daily tasks.

We did have some missteps from time-to-time, but because the team knew I was looking out for them and would defend their decisions if they could prove to me they were correct, we didn't have issues with the customer or senior management trying to butt in. The team worked hard, even on weekends without complaint, because they took ownership of their piece of the project. Eventually, the project came in on time, with just a slight cost overrun. But more importantly, the project implemented with no calculation errors, only a slight printing problem that was easily corrected.

So what did that story have to do with anything? As I stated before: *You must be able to take a business strategy, explain it clearly to your team, motivate them, execute your strategy and get outrageous results when done.* My team knew what I wanted based on my meetings with the customer and senior management. I broke the project down into easy-to-deal-with chunks, which was something nobody had thought to do before.

They knew I trusted them enough to let them handle their components in the best way they thought would work. I believed they could do the task, even though they and others had failed before. They knew I would run interference for them with the customer and senior management and they knew they could do it because I believed in them.

It may sound like hype, but being able to think about strategic plans differently (ie. transformationally), and then articulate your ideas to your team so that they have confidence in you and in where you're going to take them, is the key to having a happy, successful team who will move heaven and earth to get the job done because they believe in you.

Often thinking 'out of the box', or transformationally, is necessary to implement new technology or aggressive strategic plans. But that's not the only aspect of a manager's job. Another aspect is handling human capital. There are several parts to this.

First, the manager is responsible for her team and this includes the hiring and firing aspect of the position. To have an efficient team, all members must work together well. If they can't, then it is the manager's duty to the team to work with that person to get them back to being a team player or to terminate them and find another player who can work with the team if it becomes apparent that the person isn't a team player. This duty cannot be turned over haphazardly to a project manager or supervisor, though the manager may ask for input from these folks.

Secondly, and more importantly, a manager is responsible for the mentoring and bringing her team up to higher levels within the organization. Employees look to their manager to guide their career up the corporate ladder by giving them honest feedback and increasing levels of responsibility when the manager feels they are ready for it.

Mentoring is a crucial aspect of a manager's position and should not be taken for granted. Employees feel empowered when they are given additional respon-sibilities and this helps the overall cohesiveness of the group. Honest feedback should be given when needed, both positive and negative, so the employee can grow and learn from mistakes but also from things that they do well.

Being the strategic visionary for the department and the overseer of the human component are what define a manager. Other duties such as budgeting, efficiency, proposal writing, and customer service, come in to play, but these two are the essence of who a manager is and what they are expected to do. Next, let's take a look at the difference between a manager and a project manager.

2 THE DIFFERENCE BETWEEN A MANAGER AND A PROJECT MANAGER

Don't confuse a manager with a project manager –
they're NOT the same thing!

A Manager is transformational; a visionary.

A Project Manager is transactional; they get the
vision accomplished, and are task oriented.

A project manager has a very different role to play
in an organization. As I stated previously, a manager is
the person who takes the strategic goals of the company
and figures out how to execute them within her
organization. A manager's position is to be a visionary
and to think transformationally, in other words, thinking
of ways to do things differently to achieve much better
results than previously. She may come up with the
strategic plan individually, or be part of a team of
management that determines the strategic plan for the
overall department or organization.

Often, the manager will be looking several years ahead to determine where the organization will be headed and what will be needed to achieve that direction. They are the thinkers.

A project manager, on the other hand is task-oriented. They are the doers. They get the vision accomplished. They take the vision from the manager and determine the precise steps necessary to achieve the outcome.

While the manager and project manager must work together in harmony (remember the analogy of the conductor and the musicians), they perform two very distinct actions. A project manager should never be left to determine the strategic plans or goals of the company. That is not their function, no matter how skilled they are at getting tasks accomplished. Also, they usually aren't involved in the strategic planning process for the organization. They don't have the big picture the way the manager does. The manager, as well, should not be in the habit of getting bogged down in the minutia of individual tasks or assignments as this diverts her attention away from the big picture.

When these duties are separated out properly, the manager is free to manage the strategic goals of the organization as well as the human equation. It is unreasonable to expect the project manager to deal with personnel issues, though they may be asked to give input on the productivity of a particular person. This leaves the project manager free to do what they do best – manage tasks.

Now that we know what the manager and the project manager's roles are, the next obvious question is why can't we have one person do both? Many companies try to save money by having a project manager fulfill management duties as well. This may seem like a good cost-saving measure, but in reality it's not. It is very difficult to perform the tasks necessary to bring a project in on time and on budget while trying to manage the people, mentor them, handle the customer's expectations and create the corporate vision. Unfortunately, one duty or the other will suffer.

Getting bogged down at the task level on a project makes it difficult to see the bigger picture. Likewise, if you're working on the strategic vision, you have the ten thousand foot view of the organization so trying to bring it down to ground level then splitting objectives into individual tasks to be worked on can be nearly impossible. Going back and forth between the two can be extremely difficult and keeping the proper perspective at the proper time exhausting.

3 WHAT MAKES A GOOD MANAGER

We've all had managers at one time or another that were exceptional. Maybe we couldn't put our finger on exactly what made them good at their job, but we just knew they were. So what are the characteristics of a good manager?

Has a vision and can clearly explain how to get there. This is probably the most important quality a good manager can possess. A manager must have a vision for her department above just the normal day-to-day running of activities. This can mean implementing new technology, building new systems, creating new products, simplifying customer support etc. But even with a vision, if that vision cannot be clearly explained to the team, they won't have any confidence that the manager can get them where they're supposed to be going. The vision must be clearly articulated in easy to understand language. Keep the message simple enough for a middle schooler to understand.

Newspapers are written at a sixth grade level for a reason. Do the same thing. You only sabotage yourself when you try to use flowery or high level language (and I've heard some managers use complicated language incorrectly because they don't really understand the meaning. How embarrassing!) You should be able to explain your vision in under fifty words. Twenty-five would be better yet. If you can't, then you don't clearly understand it yet and neither will your team.

Puts people first. A good manager puts the welfare of her people above the needs of the company. Corporations are composed of people first and goods and services second. A good manager understands this and always tries to put her people's well-being first. This means making sure that they have as good a work-life balance as possible. People will do excellent work when they feel their home life is in balance. Working employees to death with no regard for their social life leaves them exhausted and angry. Once that happens, and they feel the manager has no regard for them as people, you can count on them spending their work day updating their resume and looking for another job in between surfing the internet.

Let your team know you're looking out for them and that if there is a family emergency, or a child needs to be picked up from daycare early, you're ok with letting them go early, but you expect that when they have a deadline to meet, they will come in and work. I'm not saying that you should let your people leave early every day, that's unreasonable. I've always told my employees that I'm not a clock-watcher. As long as they get their work done and it's good quality work, I don't care if they leave early to watch their son or daughter play t-ball or soccer, or go to the dentist. However, I do make it clear that when we have a project that must be completed, I expect them to act like an adult and get their work done. I've never had a complaint from them about this policy.

You may get some fallout from other managers who are micro-managers, but I let my team's work speak for itself. You should too. If people find you're actually in their corner and treat them as adults, the majority of the time they will behave as such. When you do get the odd one that abuses your generosity, be sure to act swiftly, less his or her attitude spills over to the others.

Understands the social styles of the staff. A good manager understands the different personality styles of her team and how to speak to each person in the style they understand. We'll discuss this in another chapter, but understanding and being able to communicate in the four various personality styles can be crucial to your team having a clear understanding of your strategic decisions and how you're going to get the team there.

Takes responsibility. A good manager will take responsibility when things don't go right. As a manager, you are responsible for the actions of your team, both good and bad. It's easy to place the blame on someone else when things don't go well, but because she is the leader, a good manager will take the blame, and the customer's or senior management's anger when things go wrong.

That doesn't mean that the mistake should be glossed over. If it's a problem with lack of training, then the manager is responsible for ensuring additional training is provided in the future. If it's a problem with shoddy work and/or poor testing, then a reprimand should be given and duties realigned if necessary. Worst case, an employee may need to be fired if the problem persists.

But a good manager realizes that mistakes are part of working and no matter how careful you may be, they will crop up from time to time. But the blame should never be shunted onto the team in front of customers or senior management. Reprimands and discussions about the issues should be done in private.

Respects the team as professionals. Treat them like adults. I know this seems so basic it's silly to say, but you'd be surprised (or maybe not), by how many managers treat their employee's like children who can't be trusted. They were hired to do a particular job, so the person who did the hiring had to have had enough confidence in their ability to offer them the job. You should too. Yes, people will make mistakes. That's part of learning and being human and it's unreasonable and actually childish to think that they won't. But if you respect people and treat them as adults, they will rise to the occasion.

Is humble and praising. She knows her team is the one doing the work. She's just the orchestra conductor. She makes sure that she gives credit where it's due and will often tout people on her team to senior management. She's not afraid to recommend staff for promotions, even when it's outside of her department and genuinely wishes them well. She is willing to praise even the little triumphs as well as the big ones.

Enjoys mentoring staff. A good manager is a good mentor to her staff. She takes pride in mentoring her staff to positions of increasing responsibility and enjoys watching them grow. She enjoys helping them to learn new skills and even move up the corporate ladder if they so desire. It's been stated that most corporate executives go into some sort of mentoring position when they retire because they enjoy teaching. I think this is very true. A good manager gets excited watching people grow and learn.

Tells it like it is. A good manager doesn't sugar-coat things or lie. She is honest with her people and tells them what's going on truthfully. There's nothing worse than a manager who sugar-coats the issues. It's disrespectful to the staff because it assumes they can't handle the truth. They're grown-ups and professionals. Treat them as such. People like knowing what's going on and if the manager doesn't tell them the truth, they're going to make it up over the water cooler. In order to cut the gossip out, it's best to be truthful as much as you can.

Now that doesn't mean you can tell them every little detail. Sometimes, for confidentiality's sake, certain things a manager may know, (like impending lay-offs), are not allowed to be divulged to the staff. But as much as you can, let your team know exactly what's going on, without putting your own take on things.

My team always knew they could depend on me to let them know as much as I could divulge to them. Because they knew what was going on, they were less inclined to spend time gossiping, and they were calmer on the job because they knew what was happening before most of the other teams did. They kept up their performance levels when others dropped because they knew what was going on when the other teams couldn't focus because they were conjecturing.

Has an open door policy. Your team should know they can come and talk to you at any time and not just during performance review periods. Show an interest in their hobbies or sports and what they kids are doing as well. Many managers say they have an open door policy when in actual fact they don't. They only want people to come in and talk when it's convenient for them. That's not the same thing.

An employee should feel that their manager has their best interests at heart and if they are having an issue either work-related or personally, they should feel COMFORTABLE in coming to discuss it with the manager. The manager may refer them to another department such as HR if the solution is out of the manager's control, but the employee should feel that they can at least come to the manager first. I've had to recommend an employee see an acupuncturist for a severe health issue she was having which turned out solve her the problem and save her a lot of health care fees.

If you have an attitude of caring and concern for your employees as people, they feel respected and valued and this will show in the quality of their work. Don't be afraid to spend a bit of time talking about non-work related things and always try to pick out an activity or sport that each person enjoys and talk to them about it. It helps to build rapport.

However, don't be afraid to let your team know when it isn't convenient to talk with you. Often, status reports or budgets can take a lot of time and mental focus, and at those times you need your team to be aware that as much as you'd like to chat, you simply can't. If you've been available up to this point, they'll be respectful of your time without feeling like you're dodging them.

One quick tip here: Sometimes you'll have an employee that repeatedly sucks up all your time, (we call these people 'time vampires'). This is the person that comes into your office and sits down and talks and talks and talks, seemingly oblivious to the fact that both of you have work to do.

When this happens, don't take it! That's giving her permission to interrupt you whenever she wants to chat. When you've had enough of her chatting, calmly interrupt her and let her know firmly that you have either a meeting to go to, or some customer calls to make and motion to the door. If she doesn't take the hint, walk to the door and usher her out. Don't allow this type of person to dictate how much time they suck from your day.

Is solution-oriented. By this I mean a good manager doesn't tolerate whining. If there's a problem with a task, it's ok to come in and talk about it provided you come with a solution as well. It's not acceptable to just come in and whine. Steve Jobs was famous for this at Apple.

By getting people to think about a solution to the problem BEFORE coming and complaining about it, it calms them down and often they solve the issue on their own. However, if the situation is bigger and needs a discussion, having a solution in hand gives the manager and other team members a starting point for the discussion. The solution may not be workable and may not be the final agreed-upon solution, and that's ok. It's a starting point for talks. Let the team know it's ok to complain or question things as long as they come with some kind of solution with them. It's not ok to take up the manager's time with idle whining. That's non-productive to all parties.

Knows first-hand what's going on in the department. An informed manager gets engaged in what's going on in her department. She'll walk the floor talking to people and shows an interest in their after work activities and those of their family. She remembers birthdays usually with a card and thinks of her people as an extension of her own family. When she needs something, she'll generally ask in person unless she's busy. She welcomes dialogue and even disagreements, knowing that she doesn't have all the answers. She values her team's opinions and encourages them to think out of the box, not disregarding any idea no matter how crazy it may first appear to be.

In doing this, her team feels that if the need arises, she will roll up her sleeves and work alongside them, not sequestering herself in her office and out of reach. This encourages the team to be more open and share ideas that can lead to tremendous organizational improvement.

Isn't afraid of confrontations. Disagreements are a part of working together as a team and the manager knows this. She tackles confrontations head on and quickly, knowing that the faster action is taken, the less impact it will have on the morale and output of the team. Though she may not enjoy it, she's not afraid to fire someone if their performance is continually not up to standard. This lets the team know that dead wood will not be tolerated and that performance is expected. Rather than fearing this, it brings a sense of relief to the team who know she has their best interests at heart.

This is also true when it comes to confrontations with senior management. A good manager isn't afraid to confront her superiors when the need arises. In order to make good policy decisions for a company, senior management needs an honest opinion of what's happening beneath them. Often, this may not be what they thought was going on or may not even be what they want to hear.

However, a good manager knows that being truthful is better than lying even if it's painful for her boss to hear. She's not afraid to confront senior management when the strategic decisions don't make sense, or can be harmful to the organization. Everyone can make bad decisions, therefore it's important to have the guts to confront senior management and let them know the decision is a bad one. You may not win the battle, but at least senior management is going into the decision a bit more knowledgeable about the outcome and effect than before.

Doesn't try to be everyone's friend. At first, this may seem to contradict what I said previously about taking an interest in your team's hobbies and family. However, building rapport with someone by taking that type of interest is not the same thing as trying to be everyone's friend. A manager's job is to execute the vision of the department. That means making tough decisions at times that employees may not like. However, the manager realizes that while it's nice if her employees like her, it's not a requirement. She's not there to be their friend, she's there to get work done and she expects them to perform. By making that clear, employees feel secure that she isn't going to play favourites to her friends. This also earns respect from the team.

Isn't afraid to delegate. No one person can do it all. A good manager knows this and delegates what she can to the appropriate people. Now that doesn't mean she delegates everything then sits around and surfs the internet all day. She delegates the tasks that aren't the best use of her time. Her time should be best spent on the vision for the department and how to accomplish it.

The daily running of a project, should be left up to a project manager (if there is one in the department). She is available to be consulted on issues, but gathering daily tasks and checking on progress is not the best use of her valuable time on a project. What is a better use of her time is meeting with customers, setting expectations, understanding their needs and issues to be better able to determine how her team can produce results for her customers that will enhance the customer's and the company's profitability.

Knows how to properly run a meeting. This isn't as simple as it seems. Most meetings are too long, get almost nothing done, and generally turn into a gripe fest about issues and/or people. A properly run meeting should have a specific agenda that all attendees are aware of, and they begin and end ON TIME. No excuses here.

Everyone's time is valuable. There is no reason to start a meeting late. Even if key people are not present, the meeting should begin at the appointed time. It is disrespectful to the attendees that did come on time to wait for late-comers, no matter who they are. Also, the meeting should end on time for the same reasons. People are busy and if every meeting went over by even five or ten minutes, by the end of the day, meetings have cost attendees an hour or more of their valuable day just in overruns. So a good manager is mindful and respectful of everyone's time and sticks to the schedule.

Also, a good manager ensures someone is a meeting minutes taker and submits minutes to the attendees in a timely manner. She also ensures the meeting does not veer off topic. A meeting was called for a specific purpose. Stick on topic. Don't be embarrassed to cut someone off (politely at first) if they're ranting off topic and get the meeting back on topic. Everyone will appreciate it.

There's nothing worse for a manager to hear someone make an offhanded comment after a meeting that it was such a waste of time because nothing got done. If you don't know how to run a meeting or don't feel you're assertive enough to handle it, then get someone who is capable to run the meeting for you. Don't waste people's time!

4 WHAT MAKES A BAD MANAGER

You might be thinking that this is an easy one. A bad manager is just the opposite of a good manager, right? Not so fast. It's a little grayer than that. A manager can have good points and do things right a lot of the time and still not be considered a good manager.

As I mentioned in the last chapter, one of the key points to being a good manager is the ability to have a vision and explain that vision well enough that people want to follow her to the end destination. A bad manager may have the vision but can't articulate it well enough to get her team members on board and following her. People will follow you when they BELIEVE you are leading them someplace they want to go. If you can't get them engaged in the vision, show them the direction on how you're going to get them there, they either won't follow you or they'll follow dragging their feet and dragging you down with them.

A bad manager is the corporate stooge. She believes the corporation's interests should always come before her team's. Back stabbing her employees is a standard practice. She'll say one thing to them then renege on it when she feels it's beneficial. This breeds distrust in her team. They know that her actions won't follow her words and are wary when she tells them anything.

It is difficult for a bad manager to handle people well. She plays favorites, generally to the people that have the same social style that she has or have a direct opposite style because they can easily be controlled. Staff that don't fall into those categories, she keeps at a distance, satisfied with contacting them only when necessary and generally via phone or email.

A general distrust of her staff is another symptom of a bad manager. She tends to micro-manage because she thinks of her staff as unruly children who'll abuse the system if given the chance. This type of manager usually refuses to allow any telecommuting because she can't directly supervise the employee. Time off is discouraged and she will often deride the person for wanting to take a sick day, feeling that it's cheating the company.

Office politics are played to a new level and the most important thing to her is looking good for her superiors. Credit is usually usurped by this type of manager. She's fearful of her team looking better than her and may deride them if she feels threatened.

Difficult issues and people are ignored for as long as possible. If she can, she'd prefer to move a difficult person out of her group rather than trying to deal with them. She doesn't like confrontations and tries to gloss over them as much as possible. This can demoralize the team who feel that she is letting the difficult person get away with murder.

Bad managers spend most of their day in meetings. While meetings are necessary to gather requirements and make strategic decisions, continual meetings are simply a way to hide. When a manager isn't good at handling her team, is fearful of looking bad, and/or doesn't understand the work they're doing, hiding in meetings is a way to avoid making decisions and working with the staff.

Ironically, in another scenario, a bad manager can be very hands-on. Getting too much into the nitty gritty of the job and not focusing on the big picture. Often, these types of managers were moved up to increasing levels of responsibility and feel that they can do the detail work better than their staff. This becomes frustrating for the staff because every decision will be questioned and in some cases overruled in favor of how the manager wants to do the actual work.

These managers are often behind in budgeting, strategic planning and much of the higher level work expected of a manager because they're spending all their time doing the work instead of their staff. The staff eventually give up, realizing the manager will just overrule what they did anyway and let the manager do what she wants.

It's usually easy to recognize this type of manager because their desks are usually cluttered with papers, designs, programming code etc. as all decisions have to go through them. They're also extremely stressed out and irritable because there isn't enough time in the day to do the minute detail and their actual management duties.

Often, a bad manager desperately wants everyone to like her. She tries to be friends with everyone on her team, feeling that this will help when she has to make difficult decisions or ask the team to go above and beyond (such as working on a weekend to complete a task). Unfortunately, this usually backfires. Employees are looking for someone to lead them and while they'd prefer to be friends with their manager, it's more important to them to have a manager that has their back, believes in them, and above all respects them.

Respect and friendship is not the same thing. You can respect someone and not be friendly toward them. Just look at politics throughout history. When a manager confuses the two and thinks that friendship automatically means respect, this is a critical mistake that often has severe consequences. When your team does not respect you, they won't go the extra mile for you when it counts. How many times have you heard someone say "I'll do it but I'm not doing anything extra. I'll do just what I need to and nothing more." Outstanding work demands outstanding effort, and if you team does not respect you, it will be nearly impossible to achieve outstanding results.

Finally, a manager should never complain about a customer or senior management to her subordinates. It's just plain bad manners and the sign of immaturity. If you have a manager working under you, then behind closed doors you might complain about how unreasonable a request is that the customer or senior management is making, but that's not the same as complaining about the person.

However, many bad managers whine to their team out of anger, to garner sympathy about their sorry state of affairs and look for their team to whine along with them. Business is business and often you have to work with people you don't like. However, your personal feelings about the person shouldn't affect your team. We've all read stories about famous Hollywood actors and actresses who downright hated each other off the screen, but you'd never know it from their onscreen performances. They were consummate professionals while working. A bad manager allows their personal feelings to spill over into their professional life much to the detriment of their team.

5 UNDERSTANDING SOCIAL STYLES

One of the most helpful concepts a manager can have at her disposal is a solid understanding of the personality or social styles of the people working for her. Nearly fifty years ago, psychologists discovered that people interact socially in four distinct ways or social styles. They are: Analytical, Amiable, Driving, (called 'driver' from now on), and Expressive. [2]

Many companies now test their prospective employees to determine what personality style they have to determine if they will get along with with the team they will be placed in. There are several great books on the subject: *Personality Plus* by Florence Littauer, and *Please understand Me: Character and Temperament Types* by David Keirsey, if you want to read more about the subject. Plus, there are online personality tests you can take to see what type you are if you're not sure. Let's describe each personality style in a bit of detail.

---

[2]   Taken from www.tracomcorp.com/training-products/model/style-descriptions.html

Analytical: The Analytical person values facts and figures above everything. They are generally quiet, deep thinkers and take a long time to make a decision because they analyze it from every angle. They are thorough in their work, but often don't work quickly. They like having things laid out in order and often write lists. It is comforting to them to be able to check tasks off a list when completed as it gives them a great sense of accomplishment. They are not risk takers, but rather cautious and deliberate. It takes time for them to trust people, but once they trust you, they can be very loyal.

Though often considered quiet and aloof they are actually deep thinkers. They can often come up with novel solutions because they do take the time to look at issues from every angle. Look to them to offer novel solutions to problems. Engineers, mathematicians, accountants and programmers are often Analytical personalities.

Amiable: The Amiable person is a 'people' person and cares deeply about relationships with others. They are typically described as 'nice' people. They are warm and friendly and want everyone to get along with each other. They tend to be very cooperative and are good team players.

As with analytical people, amiable people often takes their time in completing tasks because they want to make sure everyone's opinion is heard. They don't like being micro-managed and shy away from confrontations either with management or others on their team. While stressful situations are often difficult for an Amiable person, they are excellent team-builders and can help to keep the team cohesive because they genuinely care about everyone.

Expressive: The Expressive person is outgoing and gregarious. They like approval and recognition. People often call them 'the life of the party' and they love to socialize. They get excited about new things quickly but often can't focus long enough to complete tasks. They will go with the flow and opinions of people in power or that they admire, often without a lot of thought.

An Expressive person can be a great team builder as they enjoy planning fun activities and parties for the group. Keeping them motivated and on task is a challenge as their attention span wanes when they become bored.

Driver: The Driver person is an outcome-oriented person. They want the facts without the fluff and tend to make decisions quickly and usually accurately. They will cut to the bottom line in conversations and dislike micro-management or being dictated to on tasks. They focus on efficiency and productivity at the cost of personal relationships. They are often considered cold, independent and even confrontational. However, they are natural leaders and in crisis situations they will take the lead and give clear, concise directions. Many leaders within the organization will be Driver personalities.

Knowing each employee's social style can go a long way to having a cohesive team. By giving work to each person in their own personality style, a manager can usually be assured that the directives will be understood. Often, an employee complains that they didn't understand what the manager wanted when the reason is that the manager didn't relate the task in the social style of that person.

For example, Analyticals like to-do lists. They like being able to check things off in order on their to-do list, whereas, Drivers don't want the minutia or the list. They just want to know what is the end result wanted and let them figure out how to accomplish it. If you mix these two up and give the Driver a minutia to-do list with step-by-step instructions and give the Analytical just the end result and let them figure out how to accomplish it, both people will be frustrated, the analytical will be overwhelmed and the Driver will be irritated.

One thing that's helpful to do is have each employee test themselves to learn about their social style, then have the group come together and review each person's style. There are different personality tests you can use. Most corporations now use either the Briggs-Meyers test or a variation of it. If you want to use an online test, www.personalitypathways.com has an excellent Briggs-Meyers test on personality styles and you can find others online as well. I have found this is very beneficial in helping the team understand the most effective way to communicate with each other. It's beneficial to have any project managers that will interact with your group in attendance if possible.

Once the social styles are identified, distributing work becomes much easier with less confusion. There will usually be someone in the group that will vehemently disagree with the style that they have been defined as. That's fine. Let the others in the group discuss it and convince them.

During testing, you may find that most people have at least two styles that define their personality. However, people will have one, single core or main social style. It is the style that they will gravitate to when they are tired or under stress. So if you're not sure which personality style defines someone, think about how they react under pressure. That will be their core style.

Another point to understand is that everyone can at one time or another work in EVERY social style. Therefore, an amiable person can be analytical when the need arises. However, working in the social style that is not your core style can only be done for a certain length of time and it will be exhausting. For myself, I'm a Driver personality and for me to work in an Amiable style is difficult but not impossible. However, I can only do it for short bursts and then I'm totally spent. Make sure you understand this when the need arises for someone to step out of their style and work in another one. Don't expect them to do it for any length of time or the results will suffer.

I'm often asked by other managers how I am able to get my team working together without the typical misunderstandings that most teams have, especially during crunch times. By understanding their individual social styles, I'm able to assign tasks that are unambiguous and quickly understood by delivering the message in the social style that person needs.

For an Expressive person, I make the task sound like loads of fun and let them know that there will be a reward given when completed (and I do give one).

For the Analytical types, clear step-by-step instructions or a task list are best.

For the Amiable people, I let them know how this task will benefit everyone and that I'm proud of them for helping out because it's a big favour to me.

Finally, for the Driver type, I cut to the chase, let them know bottom line what I need them to do and when I expect it done. I don't give them the minutia because they don't need it. They need to know what and when and how they go about doing it is up to them.

This explaining via different social styles often raises eyebrows of managers used to micromanaging everyone in their group. However, until they try it and see how it works for themselves, it can be difficult to understand how approaching people differently can garner the best results. But seeing is believing. Try it for yourself and see the difference it makes.

Oh, by the way – knowing the social styles of your children is equally important. I have two boys who are opposites in terms of social styles. The oldest is very analytical while the youngest is very expressive. Once I learned the secret to social styles and realized their personality types, getting them to do chores was easy. The oldest needed a list that could be checked off when completed while the youngest needed to know the chores could be fun and that he'd be rewarded when done.

On vacations, the youngest didn't mind what we did. He can go with the flow anywhere, as most Expressives can. However, the Analytical child needed to know well in advance if travel plans would change.

Analyticals can't take rapid change, they don't like their world rocked so be aware of that if there is a sudden schedule change or other unexpected issue. It can be very distressing for the Analytical personality.

Let's talk about deadlines and strategic plans for a minute. Everyone handles stress differently and by now you've probably realized that the different social styles will handle stressful changes very differently. Be cognizant of this if you are in a downsizing situation (even if it does not affect your own department). It's best to call people in according to social styles and break news to them that way. For the Expressives, let them know that things may be difficult now, but they will get better and look to them to uplift the other people. They're great at always finding good out of the bad.

For the Analyticals, break news to them bit by bit and give them time to digest it. They won't be overly talkative so don't expect a lot of questions or comments from this group. They are the thinkers and it takes time for them to understand something because they look at it from every angle. It's helpful to give them tasks to be done that can be checked off a list to take their mind off things. Otherwise, they'll brood for a long time mulling things over.

The Amiables will be distressed if there are lay-offs because they want everyone to be happy. Make sure to empathize with them and let them know that even though the situation is difficult, everyone is being treated fairly. They will most likely be the most distressed of the group so be sure to have an open door policy for them to come and vent as needed. They will be the ones the team rallies behind because they do have everyone's best interests at heart. Use them as the pulse takers to check on how the other team members are handling things.

Finally, with the Drivers, cut to the chase, no fluff and let them know how things really stand. They can take it. Drivers are natural leaders so use them in this capacity as much as possible. If something needs done, let them take charge and handle it. However, be aware that they often come off as brusque and uncaring so it's best to temper them with an Amiable person to back them up.

6 HOW TO HANDLE DIFFICULT PEOPLE

Sometimes even understanding social styles isn't enough to handle certain types of people at work. Difficult people can be draining to deal with but with a few tips, you can get through it. First, think about why this person seems to be difficult to deal with. Are they a results-oriented person and demand unreasonable results? Do they demand to be the center of attention every meeting? Do they make excuses for why their work never seems to get done on time?

The first step to dealing with a difficult person is to define why they are difficult. Another factor to consider is: are they difficult to everyone or just you? If it's just you, it could be that you're approaching them in a social style that's the opposite of theirs and therefore communicating with them is difficult. However, if they appear to be difficult to deal with for everyone, then there are other issues at play.

If you seem to be the only one having an issue dealing with them, ask someone who works well with them how they approach this person. Often you'll find they are treating them in a different manner than you. Perhaps they give them a little extra attention which the person seems to crave and that's enough to handle them. Find out what they do differently than you and try it.

Ask yourself if your style of dealing with the difficult person is in conflict with their personality style. For example: if you give vague directives to an analytical person, they may waffle for a time trying to figure out exactly what you're asking them to do. To you it may appear that they are aloof and uninterested in your request or purposely stalling just to irritate you when this isn't the issue at all.

If you've reviewed how you deal with the person and it's not an issue of conflicting styles, then ask yourself what is it that is this person's 'hot' button. Are they looking for attention? Do they crave physical rewards like money or a trophy? Do they want recognition for a job well done? Do they just want to be appreciated and loved?

Often, when someone is disruptive and/or difficult to deal with it's because their key motivator is lacking. They're craving something and not getting it. Just as a baby will cry for food and attention when they aren't getting it, so will adults. If you're not sure what their motivation is, look at their desk. Often that will give you a clue as to what this person seeks. Do they proudly display their awards and certificates? Do they have lots of photos of their children? How do they dress? These will give you clues as to what motivates these people. Often, simply giving them a dose of what they're craving is enough to make them easier to work with.

If the person craves attention, get them to organize a meeting or party and let them know you picked them because they are great with people and the only person who can do the job. Be sure to also credit them again in front of their peers. This will mean a lot to them.

If the person craves recognition, find a way during a meeting to recognize them for something they've done. Give out a gift certificate or small reward. Everyone loves these types of goodies whether they admit it or not. It's a great way to motivate the team and get camaraderie going. I've often set out small challenges to my teams such as getting a prize for being the first one to turn specifications in etc. It's friendly competition and gets them motivated to work. The prizes shouldn't be expensive, that's not the goal here. The goal is recognition.

If the person is usually quiet, the WORST thing you can do is try to make that person speak out. You can't pull someone out of shyness. Sometimes they'll be quiet because they feel they don't know enough to be able to contribute to a conversation. Other times it may be that they are simply shy. Acknowledge it but have them work with someone who's a little more outgoing but not overly so otherwise, they'll retreat even more. Have them do something that doesn't require speaking such as organizing meeting minutes or being in charge of decorations at a party. Something where they feel they can contribute but in a low-key way.

If someone has a big ego (e.g. the Diva), the worst thing you can do is try to pull them off their high horse. It just won't work and you'll end up antagonizing them. Feed the ego but in small doses. If they do something really well, make a gushing comment about it and tell they how glad you are that someone as skilled as them is on your team. However, when they make a mistake, be openly disappointed about it. Let them know how surprised and disappointed you were that they made a mistake such as that because you know that they always perform at their best level. They'll be shocked at your attitude and eager to please. Often, they'll work even harder so as to not disappoint you again.

With just a bit of detective work on your part, a good understanding of the hot buttons of people and how to feed those needs, you can turn difficult people into easy-to-work-with comrades who feel you really understand them.

7 OFFICE POLITICS

I've never been a fan of office politics. I think it does more harm than good to everyone involved. Most of the time to play, you have to give up some of your morals and core beliefs and be willing to trample on anyone to get what you want, and I don't feel that's morally or socially acceptable.

I mentioned core beliefs, so let's take a look at them for a minute. Everyone has core beliefs whether you realize it or not. These are the beliefs that you hold to in any situation. Often, you may not realize what they are but you will definitely realize when you have violated one or more of them. For example, let's say one of your core beliefs is 'fair play', meaning that you feel everyone should be treated equally. If you violate this belief by purposely favoring someone over someone else for whatever reason, you will feel uneasy about it. You may not realize why you feel this way, but it's because you have violated a core belief of yours.

This can also happen when you see someone else violating what you hold as a core belief. Using the same example – someone being favored at work over another employee, you may feel distressed and angry and want to do something about it. Core beliefs are so important to us that we will respond to situations based on those beliefs whether we want to or not. If violated, we feel edgy, distressed and even angry.

Office politics often violate core beliefs on several levels. We may have to purposely betray someone else (called 'stabbing them in the back') to get ahead. Or we may receive a promotion by providing sexual or monetary favors, (yes, that still does happen). We may be asked to cover for someone when they've done something inappropriate. For most people, these are violations of their core beliefs. In other cases, we may be asked to schmooze customers or play golf with the boss because that's part of the unwritten rules at the company. It can eat away at our self respect, though we may not realize why at first.

Many people who play the office politics game for a long time may look happy, but often they are miserable inside though they have all the trappings of being successful in their career. Betraying your core beliefs for any length of time will eat away at your soul and make you miserable.

Sometimes office politics will demand that you tell the boss exactly what he wants to hear and not what's actually going on. This is another violation of most people's core values or beliefs. Our parents and school system taught us not to lie, so lying to the boss (ie. telling him what he wants to hear and not the truth) is lying. We may go along with the peer pressure and do it, but we are angry at ourselves for doing so. People complain of stress in the workplace. Often this stress is caused by a disconnect with those core beliefs which causes us to be stressed out and uneasy.

As I said, I'm a firm believer in not playing office politics. Every time I've had a new position and a new job, I've made it clear to my boss that I don't believe in playing office politics and that I will always tell him or her how things really are so if they don't want to hear the truth, don't ask me. I have yet to have a boss who didn't appreciate that candor. It's not always easy, especially when everyone else is playing the game and you're not, but I sleep better at night doing so. Often, my boss would come into my office, shut the door and tell me that everyone else is telling him what they think he wants to hear and he needs to hear the truth, which is why he's coming to me. The CEO, CIO, CFO etc., can't make good decisions if all they're hearing is what people want them to hear. They need the truth, no matter how painful it is.

As a manager you are hired to lead people and make good decisions. You can't do that based on faulty information. How many companies have gone into ruin because the guys at the top were being told everything was rosy when in actual fact the company was headed for the cliff?

If being truthful bothers you and you're afraid your boss won't like to hear it, what's the worst that could happen? He'd fire you. Big deal. It's not the end of the world. You'd leave with your dignity and self-respect intact. But more importantly, would you really want to work for a boss or a company that would fire you for telling the truth? I don't think so.

So stay out of office politics, keep your self-respect and self-esteem and you'll not only sleep better for it but you'll be respected for it as well.

8 KEEPING THE TEAM MOTIVATED

It's a fact that if you work in a company, you'll experience periods of stress. With companies downsizing, right-sizing, off-shoring and generally doing more work with less staff, the stress levels are bound to go up. So how do you keep your team pumped and motivated when they don't see any light at the end of the tunnel, (or if they do, they figure it's a train)?

First, be HONEST with them. Let them know as much as you possibly can about what's going on. That will cut down the guessing and wild scenarios that seem to pop up when everyone's gossiping. You may not, for business reasons, be able to tell them everything, but err on the side of more rather than less. They will appreciate you for it.

If you've kept a policy of trying to tell them what you can, when you can, during periods of high stress such as the rumour of lay-offs, this will help keep them calmer than other teams because they know you're the type of manager to keep them in the loop as much as possible. Your peers may not like you for this, but what's important at this point is keeping the team focused, and idle gossip is distracting.

This is also important when times are difficult. I've had to tell my team, at one point, that the company was most likely not going to make payroll next month. As much as I hated to do it, I encouraged them to update their resumes and start looking for another job, as well as promising that I'd speak to any potential new employer on their behalf. Sounds like suicide from a business perspective, but if that's really the case, there's no point in stringing employees along for another month then tossing them out on the street unprepared.

Besides being honest, try to relieve as much stress as possible from them during difficult times. Being in IT, there were many times when we worked into the night to ready software for production. Though I was a bystander in terms of not doing the actual work, I stayed with the team until the last person went home as often as I could. I was a single parent with two young boys at home, so I couldn't always be the last person out, but I would try. It is a lack of respect for your team to go home on time during a crunch period with the flippant remark of 'call me if you need me'. Stay with them, or at least as long as you possibly can.

Get dinner for your people, even if it means you pay for it out of your own pocket. You write it off on taxes or get reimbursed by the company anyway so don't be stingy. Make sure everyone has something they can eat. Don't just pick what you like. If you have a vegetarian or two in the mix, be sure to accommodate them.

If someone needs photocopying done, YOU go do it. As a manager, you're not doing the actual work, so any peripheral activities that would otherwise be distracting or breaking the flow can and should be handled by you or your project manager (if you have one on hand). It's little things like this that show your team that you respect and value them.

Be a cheerleader for your team. Toot their horn. Let people in other departments know how proud you are of their work. This is especially true with your customers, be they internal or external. Nothing will pep your team up as much as knowing you appreciate their hard work and are willing to let others know it.

This has a side benefit as well. If your team has done exceptional work in the past, and senior management and your customers know it, it becomes easier to negotiate extensions to deadlines or requests for additional materials and supplies if they know your team is good on their word. Nothing is worse than agreeing to a deadline extension then having the team waste the time and need more.

When it looks like a deadline is going to be missed, get the team together and talk about it. Bounce ideas off each other as to how they can bring the date in. Let it be their idea so they don't feel you're ramrodding it down their throats. Often, by discussion, a new idea will come out that can save time and money. So let the discussion be free unless people start getting heated or begin suppressing others' opinions. Then step in quickly and decisively.

If, after discussions, it appears there is no other recourse but to extend the deadline, make it clear to the team that this is a FAVOUR you're asking upper management or the client for, and it won't be done a second time. You're going out on a limb to support them and you expect them to hold to their word. Often, they'll stop and discuss it more then come up with an alternate date that is often more realistic than the original one they gave you.

Once you've got that revised date, go with it. But again, they need to understand that if the date slips again, they're going to have to give you something big in return if you have to go to management a second time. I've had people volunteer to work every weekend until a project is finished because I supported them for one extension and they couldn't bring themselves to ask me to go to senior management and ask for a second extension. That's power! But it's also respect. I stuck my neck out for them and they let me down and now they realize they have no right to ask me to do it a second time.

This is what separates a successful, cohesive team from an unsuccessful one. In a successful team, everyone shares the burden. The team doesn't just pawn it off on the manager as if it's her problem for them missing the date. If the date has been assigned by the customer or management and there was no input by the team on it, then as the manager, it's your responsibility to help your team with resources as much as possible to try to achieve that date.

However, if the date is simply unrealistic, gather as much input from the team as possible as to why the date is unworkable and immediately go to upper management with it. Do not go to the customer. That is upper management's responsibility. If you've talked to the customer and they still gave you this date, then let upper management handle the fallout.

Support your team as much as you can and give management as much ammunition as possible as to why the date won't work. Let them go to bat for you with the customer. But you have to let management know what IS a workable date and for that you need input from the team. Once the team gives you their best estimate date, hold them to it for as long as you can. Unexpected things may come up and the date eventually may need to be modified, but initially, hold them to the date they themselves came up with. There is pressure on them not to look bad and they'll try their best to stick to that date. Often, unless something big goes amiss or a strategy is defective, they'll usually make the date or only miss it by a little bit. But the idea that you're expecting them to hold themselves accountable to their actions goes a long way. Use it.

9 HIRING

Part of your job as a manager is to build a team. During the course of your management career, you will have to hire new employees either because you're adding staff or replacing a staff member that has left the company. There are several parts to the hiring process: Writing the job request, or 'req' for short, reviewing the resumes to select potential candidates to interview, phone interview, face-to-face interview, and finally, the offer letter.

When you get approval for a new or replacement position, it's your chance to obtain a new employee that can have additional skills your team is missing or will need for future projects. But don't get too crazy with this. First and foremost, you need someone who can do the job you need done. But if you can find someone with additional skills, that's icing on the cake. Decide what tasks this person will perform and what skill set will be needed. Do you need someone with specialized computer skills? How about WORD or EXCEL?

Whatever the major skill sets that are needed, this is what your primary requirements for the job should be. If there are additional skills that could be useful now or in the future, put these as secondary skills or 'nice to haves'.

What type of education does the position need? Be careful here. Many people have excellent skills but not necessarily the educational requirements you may desire. Take that into account. Just because someone has a Master's degree or PMP certification, doesn't mean they can do the job. But if you are in a field where specific certifications are a must, such as requiring a state teaching certification, make sure that requirement is clearly specified.

Once you have identified the requirements needed, it's time to write the requisition, or req. Normally, your Human Resources, (HR), department will have a form for this, but if not you can easily write your own.

First, give a brief description of your department and what it does, then explain what the new position would entail. Be specific. If the person would be working in a team, state that clearly.

Next, identify the skills that you are looking for in a candidate. Some managers feel it's acceptable to give the 'pie in the sky' requirements, but my personal preference is to be realistic because having lofty requirements may turn off extremely good potential candidates. I have seen programming positions asking for someone with a PhD, which is ludicrous. If someone is a typical programmer, a PhD is unnecessary and may even be counter-productive as the employee may want to spend more time designing the ideal system than getting the actual work done. I'd rather hire someone who has most of the skills I need, but is trainable on the other skills, than waiting for my 'pie-in-the-sky' candidate who never arrives.

After the skill set identification, you might want to give any specifics about the department such as work hours, dress, whether relocation payment will be provided or if only local candidates will be considered. Another thing that can be helpful to HR is to give them a list of keywords to search for in each resume. Since most recruiters and HR personnel use software programs to process applicant resumes, a list of keywords for the program to search on will help narrow down the search process.

One final point that should be obvious but I'll say it anyway - do not discriminate! Don't put anything in the request that can be construed as discriminatory, such as: "Women only", or "Latinos need not apply." If you do, HR should catch it, which will make you look foolish, and if they don't catch it, you're opening both yourself and your company up for a lawsuit. So use good judgement here.

Once you've submitted the request, HR will sift through resumes and send the most promising ones to you for review and potential interviewing. You may want to do the resume reviews in a committee made up of people that will be conducting the interview with you. This would mean a supervisor, project manager and any senior team members that would be working with the new hire.

How you determine which candidates to interview is highly subjective, but look at their address to see if they're local or out-of-state, which may mean relocation expenses if your company offers this service. Don't put too much emphasis on any work history older than ten years. If the candidate hasn't used a skill you need in the past few years, they'll probably need retraining on it anyway. Look for candidates with recent use of the skills you're looking for.

When everyone has reviewed the resumes, pick the top five or so and have HR schedule phone interviews with these candidates. If you don't have an HR department to handle this, email the candidates directly and schedule the phone interviews.

If you haven't done so before now, start building your interview questions. Since interviewing candidates isn't an everyday activity for managers, most don't know how to properly interview and don't like it. On top of all the other activities a manager has to do during the day, interviewing is an additional task that can be burdensome if you're not prepared. Interviews are normally conducted in two phases: a phone interview; and an in-person-interview afterwards. Different sets of questions should be asked at each interview.

The phone interview should last anywhere from 10 to 30 minutes. Your task here is to determine if this candidate has enough of the skill set you're looking for to come in for an in-person interview. Ask specific questions about their past experience, when they have last used the skills you're advertising, and what interests them in your advertised position.

You want to get a sense of whether this person can do the job you will need them to do. Again, what you're looking to do is get a sense of whether this person can do the job. If it doesn't look like the person will be a good fit for the position, politely end the call. Don't drag it out when it's obvious the person won't continue through the hiring process.

Prepare these questions in advance and keep them handy. You'll use them for all your candidates and when other positions open up, you can use these questions as the starting point and then modify them as needed for other positions.

Once you've completed the phone interviews, schedule the candidates that you want to continue through the process for a face-to-face interview. In this interview, you're looking to see if the candidate can work with your team. In this interview, you can ask more pointed questions concerning the position such as giving a hypothetical situation and asking the candidate how they would handle it. You're looking to see their composure and how they answer the questions.

You may want to ask several questions to determine their personality style to see how they will work within your team. Since this interview is about fitting into the team, it's best to have a few team members sit in on the interview. If the candidate will be working with someone in a mentee role, have the mentor help conduct the interview. That way they can get a sense of whether this person would be a good fit in working with them.

Again, prepare your questions in advance and keep them for future reference. The team members that will participate in the interview should also have prepared questions, and I would recommend all interviewers get together before the interview to develop questions and decide key things to look for in a candidate. You've got to hire the person but they've got to work with them so it's important for them to have a voice in the process.

For the interview, plan on anywhere from 45-90 minutes. Any longer and you're all going to be tired, plus you and your staff have your normal work to do so try to keep within that timeframe.

Prepare an outline of the interview so if you get off track discussing something else, you can refer to the outline and get back on track. You could begin by discussing the position briefly again, talk about their experience and ask them to discuss past experiences, you can also ask them to explain how those past experiences could apply to your position.

Get the other interviewers to ask hypothetical examples and how they would solve them. Do not let your staff try to get your candidate to solve an actual problem for them. That's not fair to the candidate to get them to solve an actual issue for free.

When your team is done asking questions, if you didn't ask social style questions, now's the time. You may want to ask a few questions about work habits; do they like working in a team? Alone? Can they work on weekends if necessary?

Usually, by the end of the interview, you and your team should have a pretty good indication of whether this candidate can perform the job and work with the team. Get together immediately after the interview concludes and get everyone's opinion and input on the candidate. Rate them from a 1 to 10, where 1 would be 'definitely NOT hire" and 10 would be "Can they start today?"

If anyone has specific notes about the candidate, log those as well. In this way, once all candidates have been interviewed, it's easy to go back through your notes and see which candidate is best suited to both the position and the team.

By preparing ahead of time, you can make the hiring process relatively smooth and painless and hire some excellent employees through it.

10 FIRING

Unfortunately, the flip side of hiring is firing. You may need to reduce staff because of layoffs, outsourcing, or because of poor performance. Firing is probably the most painful, gut-wrenching task a manager has to do.

The key to firing is not to drag it out and be honest without being rude, and always be empathetic. Call the person into your office or a conference room and be sure the door is closed. Explain the situation briefly and let them know they are being let go. If their work has been unsatisfactory, tell them. Everyone deserves the truth in this situation. Be brief but polite.

In both cases, give them some time to process what you've said and vent. This is the time to be empathetic. They'll appreciate it. Never call people in as a group to let them go. Each person will take it differently and you need to give them time privately with you to compose themselves.

If you've fired a single employee for performance issues, after you take any company property from them, either you or security may be required to walk them off the premises. While tempting, don't let them complete the day. It's embarrassing for them and horribly awkward for the rest of the team.

Once they've left the premises, call the team together and briefly let them know that the person was let go, but don't elaborate. The team most likely already knows the person had a performance issue without you saying anything. This should send a clear message to the rest of the staff that poor performance will not be tolerated.

If it's a layoff situation, be prepared for the staff to spend the rest of the day NOT working. It's just too stressful. Keep yourself available for people to come in to talk to you about their feelings. Many will be shocked, resentful of the company's decision, and want you to explain the company's reasoning. Be prepared for this.

For the staff that didn't get layoff notices, while relieved, they'll be wondering if there will be additional layoffs and whether they'll be next. Tell them what you've been authorized by senior management to say. Don't guess or make anything up. If you don't know anything else, say so. If you've been honest with them up to this point about what goes on in the company, they'll know you're telling them as much as you can and won't push for more. It's important at this time to manage with a light hand. Don't expect a lot of work to get done initially until people's emotions settle down. Offer as much support as you can.

While one of the most unpleasant tasks a manager has to undertake, if you handle firings and layoffs with honesty and empathy, the affected person(s) will leave with their dignity intact.

11 PERFORMANCE REVIEWS

Aside from hiring and firing, giving performance reviews is usually the most stressful thing a manager must do during the year. It can be difficult when an employee is expecting a great review and a bonus or raise and you have to break it to them that none of that will be happening. Review time is exhausting and nerve-wracking, so prepare as much in advance as you can and schedule the reviews out carefully.

If you don't already have them, create individual reports from each team member, place them in file. This will help when you are preparing reviews so that you can go back and revisit work done throughout the year. Take notes on work done well or not so well and put them in with the status reports or on a separate sheet. Weekly updates are best, but monthly will work provided you identify what projects or tasks your notes belong to.

What you're aiming for is to see some sort of progression through the year. To justify a raise to senior management, often you will have to prove the employee is worthy of it. By having these notes organized by weeks and months, you should be able to show skill and responsibility progression through the year.

If an employee is having issues either skill-wise or performance-wise, this should be clearly evident if you've been keeping notes on status reports. This will enable you to rectify the problem before it gets too far out of hand. Review time should never be the first time they've heard of a performance issue. By making notes you can track performance issues and judge if progress to improve the issue is being made.

When performance review time rolls around, get out your notes, and starting at the beginning of the year and working your way through the year, highlight the successes the employee had and also areas where the employee will need improvement. Without notes, it's difficult to remember things that happened at the beginning of the year. This way, you won't forget things that happened in Q1 or Q2. That can make the difference between someone getting a raise and not getting one or getting a larger percentage increase than might have otherwise been given.

For a performance review, show the employee how they have improved over the year, by touching on projects or tasks that show steady growth. If improvement is needed in an area, in the same way, highlight throughout the year where the employee has had issues or problems.

Being able to show specific issues an employee has had through the year removes most of the complaints the employee may have that you are making issues up or singling them out. You can also show them how they had issues at a certain point in the year but overcame them later on. Never underestimate the usefulness of keeping good performance notes!

Reviews can be stressful for both you and your staff, so don't attempt to rush through them all in one day. Allow 30 minutes or more per review and I would recommend not doing any more than two or three per day. Even at 30 minutes, if you've done three that day, that's 90 minutes of your day that you can't do your normal work. That can add up fast, especially if there are critical tasks on your plate.

Since you will be blocking out time from your normal workload to do reviews, do them in one block each day. Don't spread them out throughout the day. Mentally, you need to prepare and once you've prepped for them, get them done for that day then go back to your normal work.

During the review, always start off with the good points and the positive things the employee has accomplished throughout the year. This sets the mood for the review for both of you. You should always try to highlight one area of improvement for each employee, even if they're your top performer. Nobody's perfect and everyone can use improvement somewhere.

Discuss the areas of improvement in a positive tone. Your objective isn't to degrade the employee, but to help them to improve their work skills. Pick one area or task that you want them to work on next year (or until the next review period), or you can give them several choices and let them pick the one they want to work on. Finish the review by letting each employee know you're proud to have them on your team. They've worked hard for you throughout the year and deserve your praise during the review.

With a little work throughout the year, you can make review time less traumatic for both you and your staff. Keep good notes throughout the year so you won't forget successes at the beginning of the year or areas that needed improvement. Plan your reviews ahead of time and be sure to schedule them out to minimize your stress level.

12 RESOURCES AND EFFICIENCY

When your team trusts you, it's easier to get things running smoothly. An efficient team is a productive team. There are several aspects to efficiency we'll discuss.

Resource Analysis: Align resources to their core strengths unless they specifically tell you otherwise, and if they do, they'd better have a good reason. Typically, we as managers hire the most qualified person for the job. This means that if we are looking for an SQL programmer, for example, we're going to hire the best, most qualified SQL programmer out of the pool of candidates we have to choose from. We wouldn't hire a JAVA programmer, or a business analyst for the job. Continuing that line of reasoning, if we have a task requiring an SQL programmer, we're going to put our best person on it unless they are already on task for something else. In that case we put our number two person on it and so on down the line depending upon their workload. Align your resources to the specific tasks they are best suited for.

Resource scheduling and Workflow: Once you know who should work on what tasks, you need to figure out how to schedule these people properly. The worst thing to do is overwhelm them. Go back over prior tasks and projects and determine how long on average it took to complete these tasks.

Next, decide if this task is similar, less complicated or more complicated. Adjust your overall time frame accordingly. Therefore, if a similar task previously took four weeks to complete with two people on it, a similar task with people of a similar skill set should take approximately the same time.

Once you have these rough estimates, you can begin planning to schedule resources. However, before you do that, it's helpful to get some consensus from senior management and your customers. This involves ranking priorities for tasks. Whose task takes greatest priority?

Generally, something that is a government directive (if your industry has them) should take precedence over all other tasks. Resources should be assigned to these first. Err on the conservative side if the directive is something you haven't dealt with previously, otherwise you should have an idea of the number of resources and time frames needed.

After you have the government directives resourced out, it's up to senior management to determine what priority other tasks should have. This usually means meeting with your customer and senior management to set the priorities. Once agreed upon, the remaining resources can be aligned to tasks as necessary.

It's helpful to have a spreadsheet or project plan to track status on tasks and also allow both management and clients to re-prioritize as necessary. By having regular meetings, keeping everyone, including the team, updated on progress and allowing re-prioritization as needed everyone feels they have a stake in the process.

By aligning your best resources to the tasks they are best suited to, the full efficiency of the team can be put into play. Over time, as you review completed tasks and projects, you'll begin to get a better feel for estimating new tasks. You'll be able to properly estimate out the time needed based on how well your team works. You'll get a good feel for the capabilities (and limitations) of different team members and how much through-put they can accomplish in a certain time frame. Once you know this, it will become easier to resource tasks and you'll find that you can get more work accomplished.

For the senior members of the team, allot time to train junior members as time and tasks allow. This spreads the knowledge around the group. Cross-training is another excellent method of spreading knowledge around if you have time to do it. Let the 'expert' write notes out for the person they're cross-training and let the cross-trainee expand on those notes. Then pass them to the next group to be trained or keep them in a centralized location for easy reference.

The biggest complaint I hear from technical teams is that management never allows them time to learn other tasks within the group and people start to feel pigeon-holed into one, and only one, task. By cross-training and mentoring junior members, knowledge can be spread around and the efficiency of the team expanded.

One final note on resources – don't be afraid to ask for more. If the job requires it, ask for what you need. If you get push back but you really feel it's necessary, fight for them. Often times, senior management wants to see how serious you really are about needing them. Everyone would like to have more people and the best tools and equipment available for their team, but most give up without much of a fight when the boss says 'no'.

If you've aligned your resources well, tuned up your efficiency and still don't have enough resources to complete the tasks, you have a good case to make for asking for additional help. Sometimes this means taking the time to write a proposal to senior management. But if you've been keeping senior management in the loop on your resource scheduling meetings, and with updates on the scheduling queue, they should already know if you're really short-staffed or not.

In terms of equipment, try to make due with what you have, but if you need new equipment or additional equipment, the same rules apply. Don't be afraid to ask for it. If it's something you feel you can budget in at some point down the road, do so, but if you need it now, don't be hesitant to take the initiative and ask for forgiveness later. This is tricky and you really need to have a good grasp on what your team really needs and what they don't. Everyone would like the latest equipment, but often it's not really necessary. But if it is mission critical to the tasks, go for it and be prepared to do a lot of explaining and probably get chewed out a bit.

If you've kept senior management in the loop during resource planning sessions, they should have a good idea of what your team can accomplish so asking for additional physical resources shouldn't be a hard sell. If you don't ask, you don't get. The worst that will happen is that senior management will say 'no', but at least you tried.

13 STRENGTH-BUILDING

Building an effective team is one of the most important tasks a manager undertakes. Having a cohesive, successful team takes time, training, team talent, and excellent communication skills. You must know each individual's strengths as well as their weaknesses. These traits aren't the same as the person's personality or social style, but they may be characteristics of that social style.

There's a lot of talk today about team-building. So much so that it's almost lost any true meaning. We talk about team players and team talk and team building as if it's some new technique just recently discovered. But building a team, or 'team-building' is really just respecting your team as professionals, listening to them in earnest, supporting them and cheering them on, and helping them improve their strengths.

Notice I didn't say 'improve weaknesses'. This may sound surprising to you since most managers and corporations spend enormous amounts of money trying to improve their employees' weaknesses. Recently, there's been a shift in thinking from trying to improve weaknesses to improving and honing strengths. That's why I labeled this chapter 'strength-building'.

It's easy to pick out someone's weaknesses, and most managers still spend considerable time trying to improve their employee's weak skills. Unfortunately, a weakness will most likely always remain a weakness for several reasons.

First, the person may genuinely not have the aptitude for the skill. Trying to make someone a math whiz who really has no aptitude for math will be frustrating to both of you.

Second, the person may not like or enjoy the skill. For example, I don't like accounting. I can do it, but I don't like it, so I'm not proficient at it and really don't want to be. So rather than spending a lot of time and money trying to improve a skill set that the employee has no desire to improve or no aptitude for, it makes more sense to devote the time and resources to help them improve skills they already have an aptitude for or genuinely like. We all learn best when it's a subject we are interested in and this also applies to work skills.

Many organizations now are turning away from trying to improve weak skills, and instead devoting time and resources to improve strengths. This can include classes or mentoring to help improve their strengths.

Teams can be realigned to assign tasks to persons strong in that skill or to partner people up so that each person compliments the other. For example, in IT we often have someone write specifications, such as a business analyst, and someone program to those specifications. However, most programmers are weak in specification writing while the business analyst is often not skilled at programming. Therefore, we team a programmer up with a business analyst who can take the concept from the customer, write the specifications and work with the programmer to understand them.

So what do you do when there is a task that no-one on the team has a strength in? Evaluate the task and see if it can be redefined into a task that someone on the team has ability (ie. strength) in. If not, is there someone on the team that has some strength in that area but may not enjoy that task (ie. ability but no desire). If so, see if you can make the task rewarding to the employee. Go back to their social style and see what would motivate them to succeed in the task. If they can do it but don't like it, make it worth their while. Dangle a carrot, so-to-speak.

If that still doesn't work and you really do have a task that no-one has strength in, can you borrow someone from another team to complete the task? However, if it's a skill that will most likely be needed in the future, it might be wise to hire someone who has strength in that area.

Let me give you an example to clarify. You have a task that requires extensive technical documentation to be written. You have no-one on your team that is a good writer. The one person who does write documentation doesn't do it really well, and he also doesn't enjoy it much. You could try to get him to write it for you by coaxing him with recognition, a reward like a flex day off, or something else that would be a hot button for him.

Another option would be to see if you could borrow someone from another department who writes documentation regularly to do this one-time job for you. However, if it looks like writing technical documentation will be consistently required going forward, you would be better off hiring a technical documentation writer who has the proper writing skills who can handle your writing tasks now and into the future.

When your team knows you're going to spend time, money and effort to boost their strengths instead of their weaknesses, they'll be much more inclined to participate. No-one likes to have their weaknesses spelled out in front of everyone, but they don't mind bragging about abilities they're good at and enjoy. You'll find that by working on their strengths, they'll improve faster, enjoy the process more and become a much more valuable asset.

Should you be interested in learning more about finding your strengths and developing them, I highly recommend the book, *'Strengthsfinder'* by Tom Rath. There is an accompanying study area at: www.strengthsfinder.com where you can learn more about finding strengths and strength-based leadership.

14 RECAP

Let's review what we've discussed so far. A good manager is one who:

    a. Has a vision and can clearly explain how to get there
    b. Puts people first
    c. Understands the social styles of the staff
    d. Takes responsibility
    e. Respects the team as professionals
    f. Is humble and praising
    g. Enjoys mentoring staff
    h. Tells it like it is
    i. Has an open door policy
    j. Is solution-oriented
    k. Knows first-hand what's going on in the department
    l. Isn't afraid of confrontations
    m. Doesn't try to be everyone's friend
    n. Isn't afraid to delegate
    o. Knows how to properly run a meeting

THE MANAGER'S SURVIVAL GUIDE

Those are the key points for a manager to remember. In addition, some things a manager should work to avoid:

1) Back-stabbing anyone
2) Playing office politics
3) Micro-managing
4) Feigning ignorance of difficult people and situations
5) Being a meeting maniac
6) Trying to be friends with staff at the expense of respect
7) Complaining openly to staff
8) Going against your core belief

Learn the social styles of your staff and understand how each one is different..

Analyticals need clear instructions and a list is best. Don't leave it up to them to figure out what you want. Be specific. Give them time to digest what you want.

Expressives like to have fun. Make their tasks sound exciting. Think 'bright lights and pretty colors' because that's what they like. Be prepared to keep them on track as they get distracted easily. Let them have fun doing what they need to do whenever possible.

Amiables care about feelings. Reassure them everyone is being treated fairly and be considerate of their feelings. They consider options carefully as do

Analyticals, so give them time to do so and don't push them for a fast answer.

Finally, Drivers like to know what the end result is, so don't fluff them. Cut to the bottom line, tell them what you want and then get out of their way. Of all the personality types, they hate being micro-managed the most. If you can learn these personalities and how to spot them, you'll be miles ahead of other managers who can't seem to understand why they have issues communicating with their staff and getting work completed.

Work on developing your strengths and the strengths of your people. It's easier to improve someone's areas of strength than it is to try to improve their weak areas.

Learn and practice resource scheduling. It can be tedious at first and it will take a bit of time to get skilled at aligning your resources appropriately to get the most work done but it's a skill worth developing. By working closely with your customers and senior management, you can effectively schedule your priorities with the best people for the tasks.

Becoming a good manager is not an overnight process. It takes time and consistent effort to learn good managerial traits while dispensing with the bad ones. You'll make mistakes along the way and often take a step backwards. But stick with it! As you begin to grow, so will your confidence in your management skills. But never be afraid to ask questions or ask for help. One person can't do it all (remember what I said about managers and project managers). Find a mentor that you gel with and learn from that person.

Above all, remember that the purpose of a manager is to manager. I know it sounds simple, and in actual fact it is, but many people make it way too difficult.

Work on your communication until you can clearly explain what your strategic plans are to your kids AND THEY UNDERSTAND IT. You should be able to do it in 50 words or less.

Value your staff. They are the most precious resource you have. Treat them like adults and professionals. Let them do their work and try to stay out of their way.

Learn each person's social style and try your best to communicate with them in that style. You'll be amazed at the difference in their understanding of what you need from them.

My final piece of advice is: Enjoy the process. As the old Chinese proverb stated, "Life is a journey that begins with a single step." Keep taking that single step every day and eventually you'll look behind you and have a group of people behind you who genuinely enjoy having you as a manager, respect you, will go the extra mile for you and tell others what a wonderful manager they have. That's the highest praise you can get. You deserve it!

ABOUT THE AUTHOR

Terri Malinski graduated from Arizona State University with a degree in Computer Information Systems. She's been working in IT for over 30 years and has been in project management and executive management for over 20 years. Ms Malinski has lived in Australia, Canada, and Japan as well as the United States and worked in various industries such as aerospace, banking, health care, education and software development. She's the also author of *Daisho*, a fictional historical novel set in Japan and *The Idiot's Guide to Section One*, based on the hit television series 'La Femme Nikita'.